Leading an Inspired Life

Columbus, OH

Front Cover Courtesy of Francisco Jiménez**; 3** © Bettmann / CORBIS; **6-8** Courtesy of Francisco Jiménez; **10-11** © Bettmann / CORBIS; **13** © Ed Kashi / CORBIS; **14, Back Cover** Courtesy of Francisco Jiménez.

SRAonline.com

An Open Court Curriculum.

Printed in China.

Send all inquiries to this address:
SRA/McGraw-Hill
4400 Easton Commons
Columbus, OH 43219

ISBN: 978-0-07-608730-3
MHID: 0-07-608730-1

1 2 3 4 5 6 7 8 9 NOR 13 12 11 10 09 08 07

The McGraw·Hill Companies

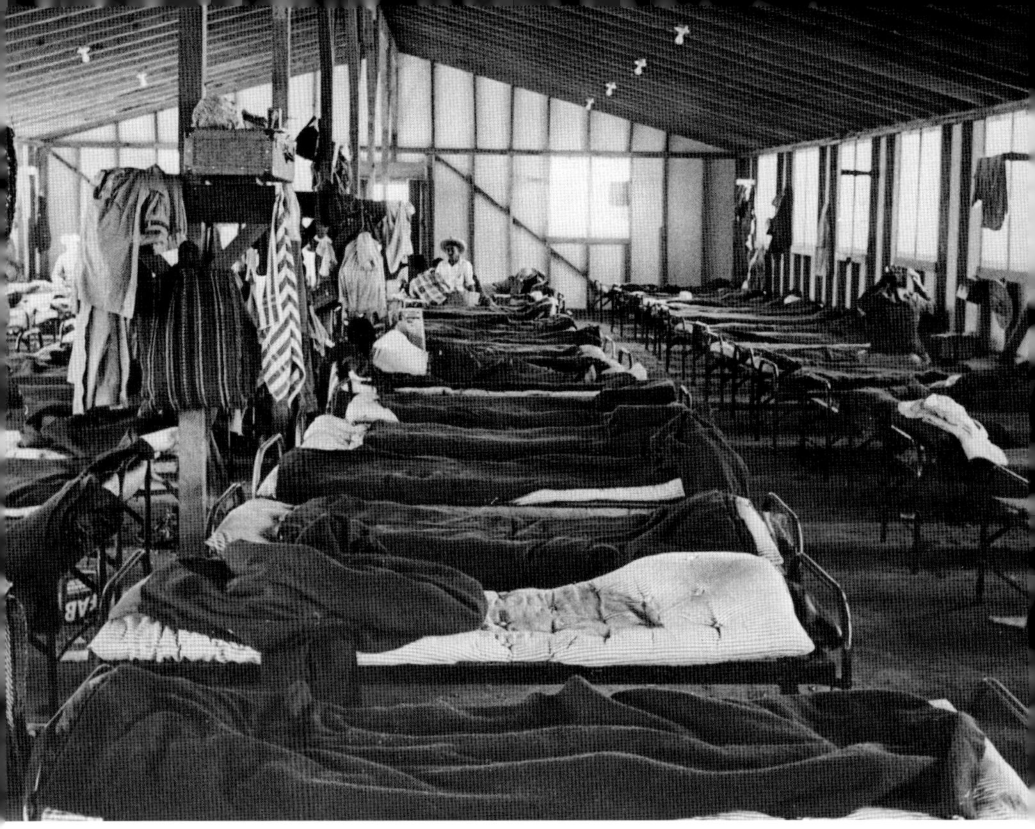

Migrant workers' camp in the 1950s

When Francisco Jiménez was four years old, he left Mexico with his father, mother, and older brother, Roberto. They left behind a poor life to come to the United States. The family entered the country through a hole under a section of fence at the border. They traveled to California, hoping to find a better life. The reality was they found life hard as migrant workers.

Migrant workers move from farm to farm. They follow the harvest. Jiménez's family picked strawberries in the summer. They picked grapes in the fall. They picked cotton in the winter.

Jiménez's family moved often among these three cities to follow the harvest.

At the age of six, Jiménez joined his family in the fields. They worked from sunup to sundown. The family earned fifteen dollars a day. They lived in shacks and tents with no running water or electricity. They always kept watch for *la migra*, the border patrol. Since the family had arrived in the States illegally, they could be deported, or sent back, to Mexico at any time.

His family remained strong. “If you work hard and are respectful,” his father often said, “you will succeed in life.” His mother inspired him, too. To this day, Jiménez remembers that even in bad times, she always had hope.

Each time his family moved with the harvest, Jiménez had to change schools. He couldn’t start school until November, after picking grapes or cotton. Because of this, he had to study more often than other students. Jiménez couldn’t speak English very well, so he wasn’t able to ask his teacher questions. And he wasn’t allowed to talk in Spanish, his family’s language.

The other children sometimes persecuted him because of his accent. At times he had to work so hard to understand the teacher that he would develop a headache. In first grade, Jiménez dreamed about the class caterpillar. He imagined that he, too, could change into a butterfly and fly away.

Jiménez as a child

The first nine years of school were difficult for Jiménez. He even had to repeat first grade. But he realized that learning was important, and he was determined to improve his English.

Jiménez found books to read that had been thrown out at the dump, including a volume of an encyclopedia. He carried a *librito*, a notebook, where he wrote down English words and their definitions. After school, while he worked in the fields, he studied the words. One day, the notebook burned in a fire, but his mother reassured him that as long as he remembered the words, all was not lost.

In sixth grade, Jiménez was inspired by his teacher, Mr. Lema. Lema tutored him in English. He helped him become more fluent, and he offered to teach him to play the trumpet. Jiménez hurried home to tell his family. He found them packing their clothes into cardboard boxes. They were getting ready to move. Once again, he had to leave school.

In 1957, Jiménez was in the eighth grade. He was getting ready to recite part of the Declaration of Independence when a border patrol officer came into his classroom. His family was soon deported to Mexico.

Jiménez with his mother and brother

Jiménez (right)
in high school

Several weeks later, Jiménez and his family came back to the United States legally and settled in Santa Maria, California. Around this time, Jiménez's father had to stop working. He had horrible back pain from his days of hard work. This meant that the family would no longer have to move around to follow the crops. Jiménez was finally able to remain in school.

Jiménez entered high school and did well. During his sophomore year, another teacher, Miss Bell, played a role in giving his life direction. In Bell's English class, Jiménez began writing about his childhood. In one essay, he wrote about his little brother, José. Jiménez wrote about the time the family lived in a migrant camp and José became sick.

After Bell read Jiménez's story, she gave him a copy of *The Grapes of Wrath* by John Steinbeck. Jiménez read it for a book report. He was awed by the story of the Joad family, who were migrant workers during the Depression years. He realized that his own story as an immigrant and his family's story as migrant workers were part of the American story just like the Joad family.

Jiménez went on to become the student president of his high school and president of the Spanish Club. He graduated in 1962 with excellent grades.

Columbia University

Before graduation, Jiménez met with his high school counselor, Mr. Penny. He told Penny that he wanted to become a teacher. Penny told him he needed to go to college to be a teacher. Jiménez knew his family did not have the money.

Penny helped him get three scholarships, and Jiménez went to Santa Clara University. Going to college was a privilege and an opportunity, but Jiménez also felt out of place. Nevertheless, he studied hard, and in 1966, he graduated with honors.

Jiménez decided to become a college professor. To do this, he needed more schooling. So from 1966 to 1972, Jiménez attended Columbia University in New York City. It was the first time he had lived in a big city. He was surrounded by strange noises and sights.

He began to write down his feelings about his past. A professor at the university asked to see his writings and encouraged Jiménez to publish his work. In 1973, his first short story, "Casa de Cartón," was published in Spanish. The title refers to the cardboard boxes the migrant families used when they moved. Jiménez says it also referred to the fragile life that they were living.

The story was soon translated into English. Jiménez changed the title to “The Circuit.” This title refers to the circles that migrant workers must travel each year, going from crop to crop.

In 1973, Jiménez began teaching at Santa Clara University. He taught courses in Latin American and Mexican literature. During his teaching years, he never forgot the difficulties of migrant work and his family’s struggles. However, he was so busy that he had little time to write his family’s story.

In 1995, Jiménez took a year off to write eleven more short stories. He talked with his family and visited places that they had lived and worked. He also thought about his past, which was often painful.

Migrant worker picking strawberries

He wrote twelve stories, one for each month. The stories became the book *The Circuit: Stories from the Life of a Migrant Child.* It won many awards. Jiménez says he wrote the book to tell his family's story, as well as the stories of all migrant workers. He feels that the people who work hard in the fields all day are all part of the American experience.

Next Jiménez wrote about his family in *Breaking Through.* The book begins when the family is sent back to Mexico. It explains how they returned to the United States, has stories about his high school years, and ends when he leaves for college.

The title refers to Jiménez's ability to "break through" his family's poverty. He believes his family's love, hard work, and faith helped him succeed.

Francisco Jiménez

He also thanked his teachers for helping him get through school by dedicating the book to them. He wrote that their "guidance and faith in my ability helped me break through many barriers."

Jiménez has also written two picture books, *La Mariposa* (*The Butterfly*) and *The Christmas Gift*. Jiménez believes in the importance of education. He is a dedicated college professor and the winner of many awards and honors. He believes that writing about Mexican American heritage is important for understanding our country. He wants children with a Hispanic background to know that their experiences are valuable and part of the American experience.

Jiménez also hopes that *all* children who read his books will think about migrant workers. "Every time we sit at the table to enjoy our meals, we should think about who made it possible to have the food we eat every day."

Vocabulary

section (sək´ shən) (page 3) *n.* A part of an area.

reality (rē al´ i tē) (page 3) *n.* Something actual or real.

inspired (in spīrd´) (page 5) *v.* Past tense of **inspire:** To stir the mind or imagination of.

persecuted (pûr´ si kūt´ əd) (page 5) *v.* Past tense of **persecute:** To treat in a cruel and unjust way.

role (rōl) (page 9) *n.* A position or function.

surrounded (sə round´ əd) (page 11) *v.* Past tense of **surround:** To be on all sides.

Comprehension Focus: Clarifying

1. Why was Jiménez's *librito* important to him? If necessary, refer to the selection to clarify your answer.
2. What was different for Jiménez's family the second time they entered the United States? If necessary, refer to the selection to clarify your answer.